First Words
School

Illustrated by
Ailie Busby

Miles Kelly

On the way!

crossing guard

car

stop
sign

walking to school

bike
rack

driver

bell

A **bike rack** is
a safe place to
store bicycles
and scooters.

bicycle

school bus

whizz

scooter

sun hat

book bag

backpack

friends

How many children are on the bus?

school

In the classroom

There are different **areas** in the classroom where we play and learn.

Can you spot a yellow car?

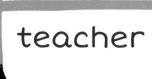
teacher

drawing pictures

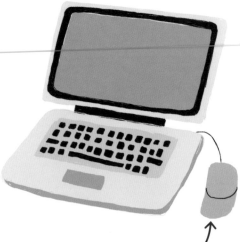
laptop

mouse

table

chair

whiteboard

letters

tablet

coat pegs

home corner

ruler

globe

5

In the playground

hopscotch

ball

To play **hopscotch** you hop into and over squares on the ground.

clapping games

buddy bench

climbing frame

slide

wheeee!

ramp

running

skipping

What games
do you like to
play outside?

skipping rope

7

In the library

story time

robot
bookcase

rug

books

How many
children are
listening to
the story?

stool

8

beanbag

book cart

carrying books

reading and writing

reading

A **library** has lots of different kinds of books.

alphabet blocks

9

Lunchtime

slice of
pizza

At lunchtime we eat together in the school **cafeteria**.

clock

lunch tray

lunchtime
assistant

serving
counter

water jug

recycling

water bottle

Can you spot a green pear?

carton of milk

cutlery station

apple

sandwich

muffin

eating together

lunch box

11

Make and do

pencil case

making models

easel

glue pot

apron

painting a picture

Can you find a model rocket?

12

paintings

It's fun to make **models** out of cardboard and other junk.

pencil sharpener

scissors

pencil

crayon

pen

monster mask

paintbrush

Making music

tambourine

trumpet

triangle

We can **sing songs** while the teacher plays piano.

piano

singing

piano keys

microphone

14

guitar

drum sticks

drum

How many instruments can you spot?

xylophone

bow

violin

recorder

music stand

maracas

15

Gym class

throwing and catching

Can you count the beanbags?

cartwheel

whistle

wheelchair

balance beam

cup

beanbags

16

Doing lots of **exercise** keeps us fit and healthy.

top

shorts

mat

backward roll

tracksuit

coach

cone

dribbling the ball

hula hoop

17

Outdoor school

teacher

helper

log

We learn all about **nature** at outdoor school.

growing vegetables

hat

trowel

bird feeder

magnifying glass

18

raincoat

den

puddle

How many different insects can you spot?

leaves

looking at bugs

boots

School fair

pony rides

tug-of-war

At the **fair** there are games, stalls and sometimes pony rides.

balloons

ice cream

toy stall

Pull, Pull!

swingboats

lemonade stall

How many children are playing tug-of-war?

barbecue

ring toss

Trip to the Farm

tractor and trailer

rabbit

At the **farm** we learn how to feed and care for some of the animals.

feeding lambs

picnic lunch

alpacas

Can you find three yellow chicks?

chickens and chicks

guinea pigs

goat

pony

23

Can you find...

book bag

ice cream

xylophone

cup

monster mask

globe

magnifying glass

lunch box

goat

pencil case

24